THE **OFFICIAL**
WEST
BROMWICH
ALBION
FOOTBALL CLUB ANNUAL **2013**

WRITTEN BY DAVE BOWLER
DESIGNED BY NICKY REGAN

A Grange Publication

© 2012. Published by Grange Communications Ltd., Edinburgh, under licence from West Bromwich Albion Football Club. Printed in the EU.

Photographs © Laurie Rampling, AMA Sports Photography, Paul Bradbury

978-1-908925-16-9

£7.99

CONTENTS

HEAD COACH

FOLLOW THAT! THAT'S THE JOB OF ALBION'S NEW HEAD COACH, STEVE CLARKE, AS HE FOLLOWS IN THE FOOTSTEPS OF THE MEN WHO CELEBRATED THE SUMMER OF 2012 BY TAKING ENGLAND TO THE EUROPEAN CHAMPIONSHIPS AND WINNING THE UEFA CHAMPIONS LEAGUE WITH CHELSEA – THAT'S ROY HODGSON AND ROBERTO DI MATTEO OF COURSE.

Steve is taking charge of a club for the first time, but after a glittering playing career with Chelsea, he's been just as successful as a coach, working as assistant to some of football's biggest names like Sir Bobby Robson, Kenny Dalglish, Gianfranco Zola, Ruud Gullit and Jose Mourinho.

And just like all of them, Steve is only after one thing – success!

"I've worked long and hard since I've stopped playing to get to this position, so I'm putting myself under more pressure than anyone else can put me under.

"The challenge is there. The last two seasons have brought 47 points so I'll be looking to get higher than that. I want to push beyond the 50-point mark.

"It's a big target to achieve – and time will tell.

"I'd be disappointed if this group of players didn't feel they were comfortable Premier League players because they've proven over the last two seasons they are.

"We have to build on that now!"

ALBION'S NEW HEAD COACH, STEVE CLARKE, WAS AT LIVERPOOL LAST SEASON, WORKING AS ASSISTANT TO KENNY DALGLISH.

NOW HE'S IN CHARGE OF THE BAGGIES, SO CAN YOU HELP HIM FIND HIS WAY TO HIS NEW HOME – THE HAWTHORNS?!

FINDING
MY WAY!

FINISH

START

WEST BROMWICH ALBION

DATE	OPPOSITION	SCORE	SCORERS	POS
Sun Aug 14	MANCHESTER UNITED	1-2	Long	--
Sat Aug 20	Chelsea (KO 5.30pm)	1-2	Long	--
Tue Aug 23	Bournemouth (League Cup 2)	4-1	Thomas, Cox, Fortune 2	--
Sun Aug 28	STOKE CITY	0-1		18
Sun Sep 11	Norwich City (KO 1.30pm)	1-0	Odemwingie	12
Sat Sep 17	Swansea City	0-3		18
Wed Sep 21	Everton (League Cup 3 KO 8pm)	1-2 aet	Brunt	--
Sat Sep 24	FULHAM	0-0		19
Sat Oct 1	Sunderland	2-2	Long, Morrison	15
Sun Oct 16	WOLVERHAMPTON WANDERERS (KO 12pm)	2-0	Brunt, Odemwingie	11
Sat Oct 22	Aston Villa	2-1	Olsson, Scharner	10
Sat Oct 29	LIVERPOOL (KO 5.30pm)	0-2		13
Sat Nov 5	Arsenal	0-3		13
Sat Nov 19	BOLTON WANDERERS	2-1	Thomas, Long	10
Sat Nov 26	TOTTENHAM HOTSPUR	1-3	Mulumbu	13
Sat Dec 3	Queens Park Rangers	1-1	Long	12
Sat Dec 10	WIGAN ATHLETIC	1-2	Reid	15
Sat Dec 17	Blackburn Rovers	2-1	Morrison, Odemwingie	13
Wed Dec 21	Newcastle United (KO 7.45pm)	3-2	Odemwingie, McAuley, Scharner	10
Mon Dec 26	MANCHESTER CITY (KO 3pm)	0-0		9
Sun Jan 1	EVERTON (KO 12.30pm)	0-1		12
Tue Jan 3	Tottenham Hotspur (KO 7.45pm)	0-1		15
Sat Jan 7	CARDIFF CITY (FAC3)	4-2	Cox 3, Odemwingie	-
Sat Jan 14	NORWICH CITY	1-2	Long	15
Sat Jan 21	Stoke City	2-1	Morrison, Dorrans	15
Sat Jan 28	NORWICH CITY (FAC4)	1-2	Fortune	--
Wed Feb 1	Fulham	1-1	Tchoyi	15
Sat Feb 4	SWANSEA CITY	1-2	Fortune	15
Sun Feb 12	Wolverhampton Wanderers (KO 1.30pm)	5-1	Odemwingie 3, Olsson, Andrews	14
Sat Feb 25	SUNDERLAND	4-0	Odemwingie 2, Morrison, Andrews	12
Sat Mar 3	CHELSEA	1-0	McAuley	9
Sun Mar 11	Manchester United (KO 2pm)	0-2		14
Sat Mar 17	Wigan Athletic	1-1	Scharner	12
Sun Mar 25	NEWCASTLE UNITED (KO 4pm)	1-3	Long	14
Sat Mar 31	Everton	0-2		14
Sat Apr 7	BLACKBURN ROVERS	3-0	Fortune, Ridgewell, og	13
Wed Apr 11	Manchester City (KO 7.45pm)	0-4		13
Sat Apr 14	QUEENS PARK RANGERS	1-0	Dorrans	13
Sun Apr 22	Liverpool (KO 4pm)	1-0	Odemwingie	10
Sun Apr 29	ASTON VILLA	0-0		10
Sun May 6	Bolton Wanderers (KO 2pm)	2-2	Brunt, Morrison	10
Sun May 13	ARSENAL	2-3	Long, Dorrans	10

The season opened with a visit from **MANCHESTER UNITED** and though we had a slow start as **ROONEY** gave them the lead, debut boy **SHANE LONG** got us on level terms soon after and from there we gave the champions as good as we got until they sneaked a late winner.

Onwards to **CHELSEA** and a late Saturday afternoon at **STAMFORD BRIDGE**. This time, we started like a train and we had Chelsea on the rack for long stretches of the game after **SHANE LONG** had broken away from the defence to give us the early lead. But even when they're struggling, **CHELSEA** have the quality to win through – even the likes of **BARCELONA** discovered that! – and **ANELKA** equalised shortly after the break, **MALOUDA** repeating the heartbreak of the week before by scoring a late winner.

A morale boosting win in the **LEAGUE CUP** at **BOURNEMOUTH** followed, but then it was **STOKE** at **THE HAWTHORNS**. That rarely ends well and once again, the **POTTERS'** hoodoo struck us down in the final minute, a mix up between **FOSTER** and **TAMAS** letting **SHOTTON** in to score the only goal of the game. Three games, no points.

ALL CHANGE FOR THE START OF THE SEASON, JUST AS IT ALWAYS IS. WE HAD BEEN BUSY IN THE SUMMER TRANSFER MARKET, THE USUAL COMINGS AND GOINGS, AND THAT MEANS IT TAKES A LITTLE WHILE FOR PLAYERS TO SETTLE IN. WHAT YOU DON'T NEED IN THOSE CIRCUMSTANCES IS FOR YOUR FIRST COUPLE OF GAMES TO BE AGAINST THE TEAMS THAT FINISHED FIRST AND SECOND THE PREVIOUS SEASON – WHICH IS EXACTLY WHAT WE GOT!

SEASON REVIEW

ADMIT ONE
105034   105034

AUGUST 2011

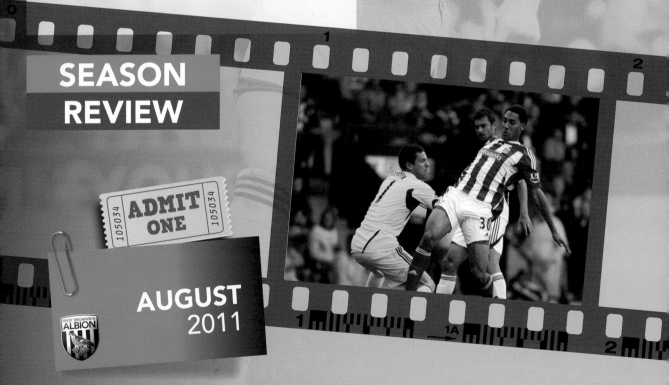

SEASON REVIEW

We travelled to **NORWICH** needing to win, and win we did. **PETER ODEMWINGIE**, who had missed the early games with injury, showed us what we'd been missing by scoring a beautifully controlled goal with virtually his first touch of the ball. True, he missed a penalty in the second half, but as we defended brilliantly against a **NORWICH** onslaught, it turned out that it didn't matter. **1-0** to the **ALBION**.

It was another trip to one of the newly promoted teams the following week, **SWANSEA** this time. We gave what was maybe our worst display of the season and were lucky to come home losing just **3-0**.

We went out of the **LEAGUE CUP** in midweek, in extra-time at **EVERTON**, then faced **FULHAM** at **THE HAWTHORNS**. It was a game where nothing much happened but that wasn't such bad news in the circumstances. A **0-0** draw restored confidence even if it meant we were only one place off the bottom after six games.

SEPTEMBER
2011

All our troubles seemed behind us just five minutes into our trip to the **STADIUM OF LIGHT** because by then, it was **SUNDERLAND 0 ALBION 2**, **JAMES MORRISON** and **LONG** putting us on our way to what looked like a mighty win. Just 21 minutes later, it was **2-2**, and that was how it finished, the **BAGGIES** reasonably happy to escape with a draw in the finish.

And so we moved on to a derby double header. **WOLVES** visited **THE HAWTHORNS** first and it only took us eight minutes to show who was boss, **CHRIS BRUNT** steaming into the box to smash in **BILLY JONES'** low cross from the left. We thoroughly controlled things from there and could have had a bag of goals, but one more was enough, **ODEMWINGIE** collecting **PAUL SCHARNER'S** backheel to drive the ball past **HENNESSEY**.

And so to **VILLA PARK**, 30 odd years since a last win there. It didn't start well, **LONG** got injured, **VILLA** scored a penalty and then **BRUNT** didn't. But with **VILLA** reduced to ten men, **JONAS OLSSON** powered in an equalising header from **BRUNT'S** corner and in the second half, **SCHARNER** cracked in a belter from another. **VILLA** vanquished!

It wasn't quite so good the week after when **LIVERPOOL** came to **THE HAWTHORNS** and won all too easily, but we were chasing up the league now, into 13th place and looking good.

SEASON REVIEW

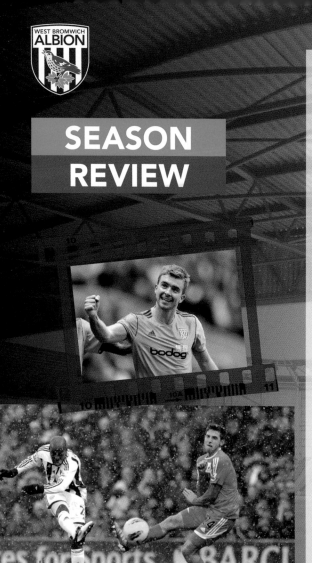

SEASON REVIEW

NOVEMBER started with good news as **ZOLTAN GERA** was finally ready to take his position in the team. He toiled manfully down at the **EMIRATES** against **ARSENAL**, but **ARSENAL** were too good for him and us and ran out **3-0** winners with a bit to spare, getting revenge for our win there the season before.

BOLTON were struggling away at the foot of the table, so beating them was crucial. **GERA** was inspired, starring in a complete **ALBION** performance that was as good as any thus far, **THOMAS** and **LONG** scoring the goals that won the game, though we could and should have won by much more than **2-1**.

SPURS were next up at **THE HAWTHORNS** and it was a sad afternoon as **GERA** limped out of the game – and the season – after 21 minutes, **ALBION** already a goal up thanks to **YOUSSOUF MULUMBU**. It was a cracking game but **SPURS**, playing the best football in the land at the time, clawed their way back into it with an **ADEBAYOR** goal almost as soon as **GERA** was gone. We held our own until the final stages when, as we pushed for a goal, the lethal pace of **TOTTENHAM** on the break brought them two late strikes and a **3-1** win.

NOVEMBER 2011

We met the third of the promoted teams at **LOFTUS ROAD** in early December. It was a tough afternoon but after **QPR** took a first half lead, up popped **LONG** late on to get us a deserved equaliser.

It was as well we got that point because our poor home results continued the week after when struggling **WIGAN** won **2-1** in **WEST BROMWICH**, despite a beautiful free-kick from **STEVEN REID** that was a "Goal of the Season" contender.

We'd dropped to 15th and were looking nervously over our shoulders as we had two tough away trips in the week before Christmas. It was a hostile atmosphere up at **BLACKBURN** and it got even more so when **MORRISON** got the actual "Goal of the Season" in the second half with a vicious volley. After **ROVERS** had drawn level, **ODEMWINGIE** made sure we took all the points with a beauty of his own in the last minute.

Then it was midweek in **NEWCASTLE** and perhaps the best game of the season, one that went back and forth, **ALBION** twice in the lead, through **ODEMWINGIE** and **MCAULEY**, twice equalised with **BA** goals, **FOSTER** making a couple of superb saves to keep us in the game before **SCHARNER** won the game with a swift break in the 85th minute. **CLASSIC!**

MANCHESTER CITY were the last visitors of 2011, and **ALBION** were expected to be well beaten by a side that couldn't stop scoring goals. But we dug in and the players went off to a standing ovation after a **0-0** draw that took us up to 9th.

DECEMBER 2011

SEASON REVIEW

SEASON REVIEW

JANUARY 2012

From the game of the season at **NEWCASTLE**, we had the worst one at home to **EVERTON** on New Year's Day! It got even worse in the last few minutes when the visitors took all three points thanks to an **ANICHEBE** goal.

Forty-eight hours later and we were at **WHITE HART LANE** with a team decimated by illness and injury, young **GEORGE THORNE** getting his first **ALBION** start and performing superbly as we made life difficult for **TOTTENHAM**. Not quite difficult enough though because after 63 minutes, **DEFOE** got the only goal of the game.

We had to work pretty hard before we got the better of **CARDIFF** in the FA Cup, **SIMON COX** registering a hat-trick in the **4-2** win, but we were back to our usual home form a week later when a **NORWICH** smash and grab raid saw us beaten **2-1**, a week before we had to go to **STOKE**.

Usually, we'd be better off going to the moon, but having won at **VILLA** and **NEWCASTLE** for the first time in decades, why not do the same at **STOKE**? So we did! **MORRISON** gave us the lead in a game where we were clearly the better team but it looked as if it was going to be the same old story when **JEROME** equalised in the 86th minute. But we kept going and in the final moments, **GRAHAM DORRANS'** free-kick from out wide found its way through the penalty area and into the far corner of the net. Result – at last!

And then we had a repeat of the league game against **NORWICH** in the FA Cup, **ALBION 2-1** losers in a game that was a replica of the one from a fortnight earlier.

FEBRUARY 2012

SEASON REVIEW

The dreadful run of results at **THE HAWTHORNS** continued against **SWANSEA**. As the snow raged around the ground to give the most treacherous of conditions, we finally struggled into a 54th minute lead and looked to be on our way. That dream lasted 60 seconds, **SIGURDSSON** equalising almost instantly, **GRAHAM** winning the game four minutes later.

It meant we still had our eyes on the relegation scrap as we went to **MOLINEUX** a week later. At the end of the 90 minutes, we no longer had any worries! We dismantled the home team, winning **5-1** when we might have won 15-1, **ODEMWINGIE** registering a hat-trick, **OLSSON** and **KEITH ANDREWS** also scoring as we not only pushed ourselves clear of danger but destroyed **WOLVES'** hopes of survival into the bargain.

With the team in a confident mood, we were every bit as devastating a fortnight later as we took **SUNDERLAND** to pieces to finally lay our Hawthorns hoodoo, beating Martin O'Neill's team 4-0, **ODEMWINGIE** scoring two more, **MORRISON** and **ANDREWS** also getting in on the act.

SEASON REVIEW

We'd never taken as much as a point off **CHELSEA** in 11 Premier League attempts, but this time it was going to be different. With **CHELSEA** struggling to keep pace with the **MANCHESTER** clubs at the top, we gave them a very difficult afternoon, two evenly matched teams fighting it out until, with eight minutes left, **GARETH MCAULEY** stabbed in the winner.

It was a bit different a week later because **MANCHESTER UNITED** were in good form at **OLD TRAFFORD**. We were only a goal down early in the second half but when **OLSSON** was sent off, our hopes of salvaging a draw went with him.

A week later, **WIGAN** played even better than **UNITED** had and had us under siege. They could have scored four or five in that time but didn't take the lead until the 54th minute. Inevitably, the returning **PAUL SCHARNER** had the last word and snatched an equaliser that we could scarcely believe we'd got, an important point as the month ended with us beaten in successive games by **NEWCASTLE** and then **EVERTON**.

MARCH 2012

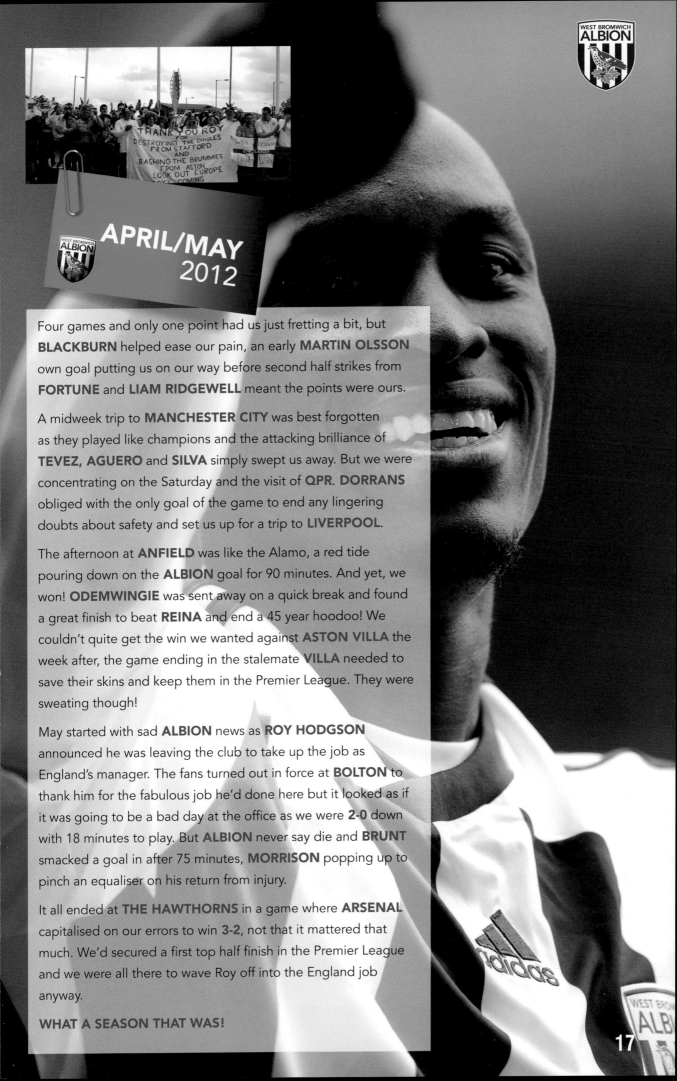

APRIL/MAY 2012

Four games and only one point had us just fretting a bit, but **BLACKBURN** helped ease our pain, an early **MARTIN OLSSON** own goal putting us on our way before second half strikes from **FORTUNE** and **LIAM RIDGEWELL** meant the points were ours.

A midweek trip to **MANCHESTER CITY** was best forgotten as they played like champions and the attacking brilliance of **TEVEZ, AGUERO** and **SILVA** simply swept us away. But we were concentrating on the Saturday and the visit of **QPR. DORRANS** obliged with the only goal of the game to end any lingering doubts about safety and set us up for a trip to **LIVERPOOL**.

The afternoon at **ANFIELD** was like the Alamo, a red tide pouring down on the **ALBION** goal for 90 minutes. And yet, we won! **ODEMWINGIE** was sent away on a quick break and found a great finish to beat **REINA** and end a 45 year hoodoo! We couldn't quite get the win we wanted against **ASTON VILLA** the week after, the game ending in the stalemate **VILLA** needed to save their skins and keep them in the Premier League. They were sweating though!

May started with sad **ALBION** news as **ROY HODGSON** announced he was leaving the club to take up the job as England's manager. The fans turned out in force at **BOLTON** to thank him for the fabulous job he'd done here but it looked as if it was going to be a bad day at the office as we were **2-0** down with 18 minutes to play. But **ALBION** never say die and **BRUNT** smacked a goal in after 75 minutes, **MORRISON** popping up to pinch an equaliser on his return from injury.

It all ended at **THE HAWTHORNS** in a game where **ARSENAL** capitalised on our errors to win **3-2**, not that it mattered that much. We'd secured a first top half finish in the Premier League and we were all there to wave Roy off into the England job anyway.

WHAT A SEASON THAT WAS!

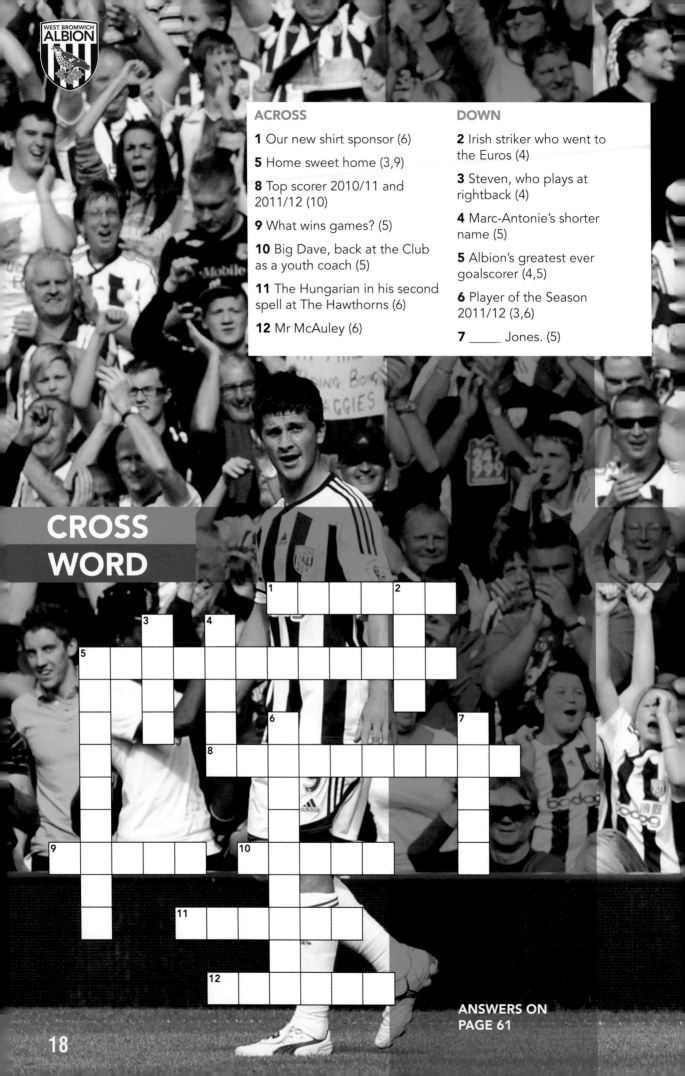

ACROSS

1 Our new shirt sponsor (6)

5 Home sweet home (3,9)

8 Top scorer 2010/11 and 2011/12 (10)

9 What wins games? (5)

10 Big Dave, back at the Club as a youth coach (5)

11 The Hungarian in his second spell at The Hawthorns (6)

12 Mr McAuley (6)

DOWN

2 Irish striker who went to the Euros (4)

3 Steven, who plays at rightback (4)

4 Marc-Antonie's shorter name (5)

5 Albion's greatest ever goalscorer (4,5)

6 Player of the Season 2011/12 (3,9)

7 _____ Jones. (5)

CROSS WORD

ANSWERS ON PAGE 61

18

When we selflessly stood aside and allowed England to take Roy Hodgson away from us because his country needed him, it wasn't the first time that a man with impeccable Albion connections had been called to the highest job in the land – it's more important than being Prime Minister isn't it?

Actually, Sir Bobby Robson once referred to being England manager as being the Prime Minister of football, and he should know because for eight years, from 1982-1990, he had the job.

He was pretty successful too, taking England to the quarter-finals of the Wold Cup in 1986 before we lost to the Hand of God, then to the semi-finals in 1990 before we lost on penalties.

Sir Bobby was a great Albion player in his day, which must account for his England success. On top of that, just to be on the safe side, he took Don Howe with him as his assistant. The two played together through the late 1950s and early '60s at The Hawthorns.

With 636 Albion games between them, no wonder they were so good for England!

YOUR COUNTRY NEEDS YOU!

There was plenty of Albion involvement at the European Championships in Poland and Ukraine over the summer of 2012, with Albion figures of the present and the recent past all making their mark.

The biggest Albion contingent wore the green of the Republic of Ireland as they did battle with the toughest group of them all, featuring Spain, Italy and Croatia. Keith Andrews started all three games for the Irish and was described as one of their most consistent performers by many as they were beaten by their opponents.

Simon Cox and Shane Long also featured, Coxy starting against the Spaniards and coming on as a substitute in the two other games, Shane appearing from the bench against both Croatia and Italy, great experience for both of them at their first major international tournament.

ALBION AT THE EUROS

It was a first for Jonas Olsson too, the giant Swedish centre-half, missing their opening game but appearing against England where he might have bagged their second goal if Mellberg hadn't got to the ball first! Jonas also played in their final group game, against France, as Sweden won a consolation victory.

And then there was England. Roy Hodgson took charge of the Three Lions after completing the season with the Throstles, and piloted England to the top of their group and a quarter-final meeting with Italy.

After two gruelling hours of football, it came down to penalties – and we all know what happened next!

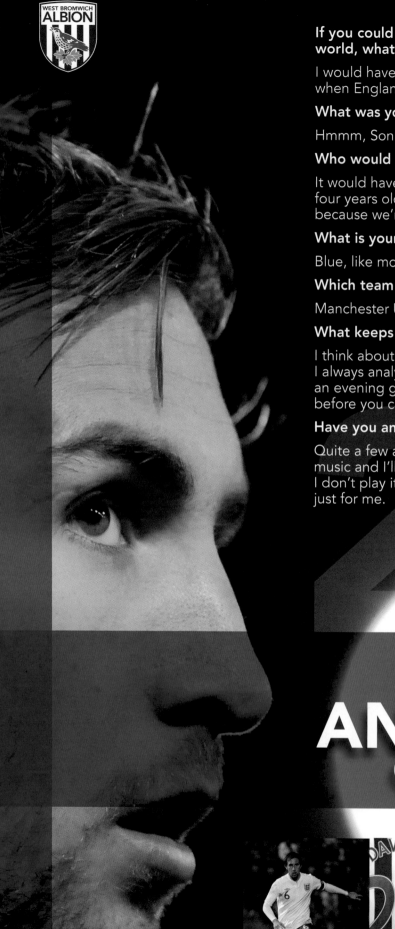

If you could buy a ticket to any event in the world, what would it be?

I would have to say the 1966 World Cup Final when England won.

What was your favourite childhood game/toy?

Hmmm, Sonic the Hedgehog on Sega Mega-drive.

Who would play you in the film of your life?

It would have to be my brother Andrew. He's four years older than me and knows me the best because we're very close.

What is your favourite colour?

Blue, like most boys I suppose.

Which team did you support as a boy?

Manchester United because my dad is a big fan.

What keeps you awake at night?

I think about the game or the day's training session. I always analyse my own performance and after an evening game you always need to wind down before you can finally sleep.

Have you any pre-match rituals?

Quite a few actually. I have to listen to the same music and I'll listen to that all the way through. I don't play it in the dressing room though, it's just for me.

ASK ME ANOTHER:
CRAIG DAWSON

Peter became the first Albion player to reach double figures in a Premier League season on two separate occasions and is our top Premiership scorer with 25 goals in all.

There were some vital ones again last season, including the winners at Norwich City, Blackburn Rovers and Liverpool.

And don't forget his hat-trick at Molineux – as if you could!

PETER PERFECT!

FOR THE SECOND SEASON RUNNING, IT WAS ALBION'S NIGERIAN STRIKER, PETER ODEMWINGIE, WHO TOPPED THE GOAL SCORING CHARTS FOR THE THROSTLES, WITH 11 GOALS IN TOTAL.

Football always throws up weird, quirky statistics, strange unbeaten runs and the like. But there are also those long, long spells without success against certain teams, or at certain venues. But last season, we decided enough was enough!

We started ticking off the milestones as early as October when we went to Villa Park, where we hadn't won since 1982 (1-0 in the League Cup), and not since 1979 in the league. It didn't look good as we went behind and missed a penalty, but we ended up 2-1 winners and made sure that we let the locals know about it!

We hadn't won at Blackburn's Ewood Park since February 1991, but just before last Christmas, a 2-1 win was ours. We followed that up three days later by going to Newcastle, where we hadn't won a league game since September 1977. We soon changed that, with an epic 3-2 victory.

We never beat Stoke, do we? We do now! In January, we won at the Britannia Stadium for the first time, our 2-1 victory the first in Stoke since September 1982 at their old Victoria Ground.

Were we finished? No. After getting our first ever Premier League point at Fulham, we then got our first ever Premiership point off Chelsea. Better yet, we got all three, beating them 1-0 at The Hawthorns in March, Gareth McAuley getting the goal that gave us our first league win over them since March 1979.

And to finish it all off with a bang, we went to Anfield, where we had not won in exactly 45 years to the day. Jeff Astle got the only goal of the game on 22 April 1967 and 45 years on, Peter Odemwingie repeated the trick. Hoodoo voodoo indeed!

HOODOO VOODOO!

THE 2011/12 SEASON WAS A PRETTY SPECIAL ONE IN ALBION HISTORY AS WE SET ABOUT BREAKING RECORDS WHEREVER WE WENT.

If you could buy a ticket to any event in the world, what would it be?

I would love to have watched the 'Rumble in the Jungle', the fight between Foreman and Ali. I like watching boxing and that fight took place in the city where I was born, Kinshasa.

Who would play you in the film of your life?

Denzel Washington of course.

Who did you have a schoolboy crush on?

Let me think, I can't remember her name... Naomi Campbell, that's it!

Which team did you support as a boy?

Marseille because of my dad.

What song would you sing if ordered to take part in a Karaoke?

'Mulumbu, wo-o-o-o, Mulumbu, wo-o-o-o!' The one the fans sing, it's easy!

What would your superpower be?

I would like to be able to fly.

What is your favourite item of clothing?

Shoes! Always shoes, I have a lot of shoes, mainly trainers though.

ASK ME ANOTHER:
YOUSSOUF MULUMBU

YOUNG PLAYER OF THE SEASON

IT WAS A VERY SUCCESSFUL END TO LAST SEASON FOR EIGHTEEN YEAR OLD DONERVON DANIELS WHO PICKED UP NOT ONE AWARD, BUT TWO!

It started in April when he was part of the young Albion outfit that beat Solihull Moors to win the Birmingham Senior Cup at The Hawthorns, fitting reward for a team that had slogged their way through the competition against all kinds of sides, at all kinds of venues, in all types of weather.

The imposing centre-half, who was rewarded with his first professional contract earlier in the season, wasn't finished there though.

On the final day of the season, as Albion took on Arsenal, Donervon was announced as the winner of the club's Young Player of the Season award.

It's just a shame he wasn't there to pick up the trophy!

SPOT
THE
BALL

IT LOOKS AS IF BILLY JONES HAS HEADED THE
BALL SO HARD THAT IT'S SPLIT INTO FIVE...
BUT ACTUALLY, OUR ARTIST HAS HIDDEN IT AND
IT'S UP TO YOU TO FIND IT FOR BILLY AGAIN!
WHERE DO YOU THINK IT SHOULD BE?

**ANSWER ON
PAGE 61**

The 29 year old Swede has scored goals in Germany, Spain and Holland in the past, but now he's after scaring English defenders to death!

"I had a lot of offers but I have never played in the Premier League. I have played in a lot of leagues – but not this one – and it was something I really wanted to try.

"Then I met both Dan Ashworth and Steve Clarke and they both talked a lot about the system and how they want to use me. I like the way Albion play with the ball on the ground because you are always afraid some English teams play long balls.

"My game is best when the ball comes through the midfield and they try and find the strikers. I try to keep the ball on the ground and I'm pretty fast. I don't like so many balls in the air but over the years I have become a better target player".

Markus' decision to come to the Black Country also had plenty to do with a fellow countryman who is now an Albion legend, as he admits.

"I talked with my friend Jonas Olsson a lot, and he had positive things to say about the club. It was an easy decision in the end. It was always a dream to come here and it's a great league for Swedish players as we grow up watching it.

"It's also nice to have a fellow Swede here. He's a good friend and comes from the same part of Sweden as me. We were also together at the European Championships."

And if Markus gets homesick, there's always Ikea just down the road in Wednesbury!

MAKING HIS MARKUS!

IF THREATENING OPPOSITION DEFENCES WITH ODEMWINGIE, LONG AND FORTUNE WASN'T ENOUGH, ALBION ADDED TO THEIR FIREPOWER IN THE SUMMER WITH THE SIGNING OF MARKUS ROSENBERG.

"It's nice to have a second Paralympics to look forward to because I was out in Beijing four years ago and really enjoyed the experience. Strangely enough, I was competing in judo out there.

"Going out to China was great, a phenomenal experience because the people there were just great, they came across as so genuine and interested in us. I was surprised how much they knew about Britain, they were very friendly and pleased to have us there.

"There were 8 or 9,000 people watching and when you're not used to it, it is really difficult to keep the right level of concentration and focus. They were all stamping their feet and screaming and shouting and I found it hard to block that out.

"This time around, it was football and, of course, in my home country. It literally is a once in a lifetime experience because it's more than 60 years since the last one here, but funny enough, I was really relaxed about it.

"In Beijing, it was a bit difficult for your family and friends to come! This time instead of a nine hour flight, it's a couple of hours down the motorway!

"It was great timing too because I'm playing maybe better than I've ever played, which is strange given I'm supposedly in the twilight of my career!

"It was just a fabulous opportunity and I'm delighted I had the chance to represent my country, my family and Sporting Club Albion as well!"

ONCE – OR TWICE – IN A LIFETIME

SPORTING CLUB ALBION WERE WELL REPRESENTED AT THE 2012 LONDON PARALYMPICS AFTER DARREN HARRIS WAS SELECTED IN THE PARALYMPIC BLIND GB 5-A-SIDE SQUAD. FOR DARREN, IT'S A SECOND SUCCESSIVE PARALYMPICS, THOUGH OUT IN CHINA IN 2008, IT WAS ALL A BIT DIFFERENT AS HE EXPLAINS.

It was only right that the Albion should play their part in it all, and, as well as the torch passing through the home of football – West Bromwich, obviously – one of our greatest supporters did his bit by carrying the torch.

"Blind Dave" Heeley carried the torch through Stoke-On-Trent, presumably as part of the celebrations, after we finally won there in January 2012!

Dave has raised hundreds of thousands of pounds for charity and is an ambassador for the Albion Foundation.

Last year Dave completed his Top2Toe challenge, in which he ran ten marathons and cycled more than 800 miles from John O'Groats to Land's End in only ten days, in aid of Macmillan Cancer Support, and in 2008 he became the first blind person to run seven marathons in seven days on seven different continents.

But Dave insisted running a leg of the Olympic torch relay is one of the highlights of his athletic career.

"It was an honour and a privilege to be involved and I think that everybody, including the other 7,999 people, must all feel the same," he said.

"It is never going to happen to me again. I'm never going to see an Olympic Games in this country again and I'm never, ever, going to be able to carry the Olympic torch again.

"I ran the 300 metres with Seamus my guide dog. I think I was the third person to run the relay with a guide dog, so it's nice for a Baggies fan to make it a hat-trick.

"Instead of an Odemwingie hat-trick against the Wolves it's a Seamus hat-trick for guide dogs in the Olympic torch relay!"

CARRYING THE TORCH

STOP THIEF!

STEVE CLARKE IS PROUDLY HOLDING UP AN ALBION SHIRT, BUT SOMEBODY'S PINCHED THE COLOURS! CAN YOU SAVE THE DAY AND DESIGN US A NEW KIT – QUICK, BEFORE ANYONE NOTICES!

If you could buy a ticket to any event in the world, what would it be?

I would love to go to the Superbowl. I wouldn't mind who was playing. I'd just love to be there for the experience.

If you were Prime Minister, what one change would you make to the country?

That is a good question. I would like there to be more jobs for people but that is much easier said than done.

What was your favourite childhood game/ toy?

It was on one of the early consoles – Sonic the Hedgehog on the Sega Megadrive, I think.

What is your favourite colour?

Blue. It doesn't have any special significance. I've just always liked it. It is a mild colour, not like red which is quite aggressive.

Who was your first-ever 11-a-side football match for and in what position?

It was when I was young boy at school, when I first started playing football. I must have been about seven years old and I played at centre-back, believe it or not.

What is your favourite other sport?

Basketball. I enjoy watching it and playing it – and I'm quite good! I can slam dunk the ball, too.

Who did you have a schoolboy crush on?

No-one. All I thought about was football!

ASK ME ANOTHER:
MARC-ANTOINE FORTUNE

FIVE-ONE TO THE ALBION!

WE'VE ENJOYED SOME PRETTY GOOD DAYS AGAINST THE WOLVES OVER THE LAST FEW YEARS HAVEN'T WE? WE BEAT THEM TO PROMOTION TO THE PREMIER LEAGUE IN 2002; WE SAW THEM OFF IN THE PLAY-OFFS OF 2007 AS WELL AS BEATING THEM IN THE FA CUP THAT SEASON AND WE BEAT THEM AT MOLINEUX AS WE EDGED CLOSER TO WINNING PROMOTION THE FOLLOWING YEAR.

But fun as all those days were, there hasn't been much to compare with our visit to Wolverhampton in February 2012.

Before the game, things were still very tight at the bottom of the table, making it an absolutely vital game for both teams, one we had to win. Win we did – and how!

The tale of the 90 minutes went like this:

34 MINS: After controlling the game and forcing some great saves from Hennessey, Albion finally went ahead when Peter Odemwingie smashed in a 20 yarder. 1-0.

45 MINS: From nowhere, Wolves equalised with their first chance. 1-1.

64 MINS: Gareth McAuley's looping header hit the back post but Jonas Olsson was quickest to react to the loose ball, firing us back into the lead. 2-1.

77 MINS: Game over when Olsson backheeled the ball to Odemwingie to score from eight yards out. 3-1.

85 MINS: Great work from James Morrison set up Keith Andrews to drive a 20 yarder in on his return to his former club and get the party started! 4-1.

88 MINS: Another cross from Morrison, Odemwingie stabbing the ball home to complete his hat-trick. 5-1.

Two days before St Valentine's Day, it was a Molineux Massacre!

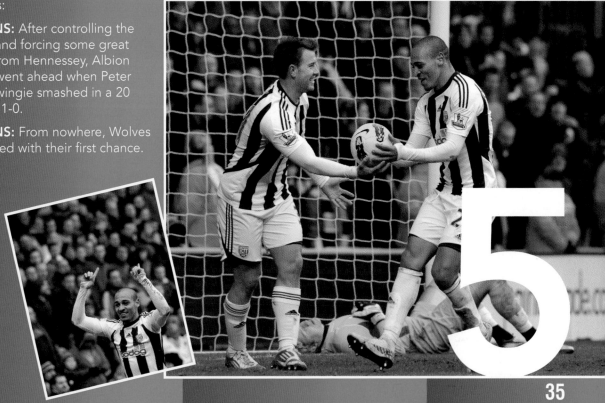

C	L	A	R	K	E	N	S	B	C	S
F	W	L	G	A	T	B	M	N	Y	H
K	T	B	I	J	O	N	E	S	U	A
G	G	I	S	A	K	F	T	E	X	N
R	L	O	Y	M	O	D	H	V	G	E
A	X	N	K	E	D	M	W	Q	K	Y
H	A	U	R	S	B	Y	I	K	D	C
A	M	N	E	L	R	L	C	Y	E	M
M	C	F	W	R	U	S	K	C	Q	U
E	U	A	B	W	N	T	H	B	O	H
L	F	H	A	W	T	H	O	R	N	S

ALBION

BRUNT

CLARKE

GRAHAM

HAWTHORNS

JAMES

JONES

SHANE

SMETHWICK

WBA

ANSWERS ON PAGE 61

LOST FOR WORDS!

THESE TWO FAMOUS BAGGIES AREN'T USUALLY SHORT OF A WORD OR TWO, BUT ADRIAN AND FRANK HAVE MISPLACED A FEW CHOICE ALBION PHRASES. CAN YOU HELP THEM TRACK THEM DOWN?

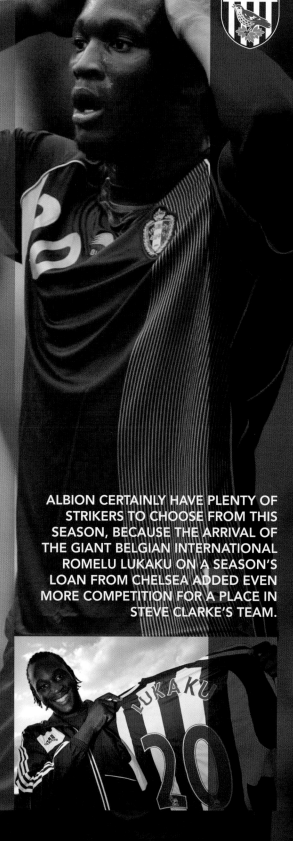

The 19-year-old striker, who joined Chelsea for £18million, decided to choose Albion as his destination this year after Steve Clarke made it clear he was part of his plans – and after Roberto Di Matteo told him The Hawthorns is the place to be!

"Since the first day I spoke to Chelsea about going out on loan, I've spoken to the gaffer here a lot. He was the first person who contacted me and that means a lot. He's been speaking to me every week since – even when I was in America with Chelsea – asking me about my situation.

"When you have a gaffer like that who has a desire to bring you to his club, as a young man, you feel confident to make the step into the unknown, because I don't know the Birmingham area that well.

"But I believe that will be good for my development as a young man and I'm very happy to be here. This club really convinced me a lot, also with the stadium and the fans.

"I heard lots of positives about the club from Roberto Di Matteo and Eddie Newton. They really convinced me to come here. Frank Lampard and John Terry also spoke highly about the gaffer. When you get that advice as a young player, you listen and hopefully this is a good step for my career.

"I already know a lot of about the team. West Brom have given Chelsea some difficult games over the last couple of seasons. This is a good team where I can learn. I want to work hard and learn a lot. It will be good for my development as a young man.

"Before I signed, I watched a lot of West Brom's games and I know they're a good footballing team. They have exciting players – the likes of Thomas, Morrison and Long, who scored a lot of goals last season. They've also got good defenders like Steven Reid and Jonas Olsson.

"I want to finish as high as possible with the club next season and score goals. Hopefully we will have a great season and keep the fans happy week in, week out".

We hope so too Romelu!

ALBION CERTAINLY HAVE PLENTY OF STRIKERS TO CHOOSE FROM THIS SEASON, BECAUSE THE ARRIVAL OF THE GIANT BELGIAN INTERNATIONAL ROMELU LUKAKU ON A SEASON'S LOAN FROM CHELSEA ADDED EVEN MORE COMPETITION FOR A PLACE IN STEVE CLARKE'S TEAM.

ROMELU WASN'T BUILT IN A DAY!

1. Which Albion number 1 was in goal for the 1968 FA Cup Final?

2. Albion have done only one league and cup double. When?

3. Jonas Olsson has been Albion's regular number 3 in recent times, but where did we buy him from?

4. Tony Brown often wore number four. How many goals did he score for us?

5. Who scored a hat-trick when we beat Wolves 5-1 in 2011/12?

6. Liam Ridgewell is our number six. Which other two midlands clubs has he played for?

7. 2012/13 will be our seventh Premiership season. Who scored our first Premier League goal?

8. We've never won more than eight homes games in a Premiership season – true or false?

9. Jeff Astle is one of our most famous number nines. How many England caps did he get?

10. We've been in 10 FA Cup finals. How many have we won?

11. Laurie Cunningham was a famous number 11 for Albion. Who did we sell him to?

12. Albion were the first club to use a substitute in an FA Cup Final. Who was he?

13. Number 13 didn't have much luck against Arsenal in the last game of 2011/12. Who was he?

14. Jerome Thomas started his career where?

15. Fifteen goals in a season is a record for an Albion player in the Premiership – true or false?

16. Where did Scott Allan spend the last couple of months of 2011/12 on loan?

17. Graham Dorrans has scored how many Premiership goals for Albion?

18. Albion were formed in the 1800s. But which year?

19. How many of our 19 opponents in 2011/12 had we never beaten in the Premiership before the season started?

20. Who was Albion captain when we won the league for the first time in 1919/20?

THE NUMBERS GAME!

ANSWERS ON
PAGE 61

AFTER ALBION FOUNDATION AMBASSADOR, BLIND DAVE HEELEY, GOT TO CARRY THE OLYMPIC TORCH THROUGH STOKE, LATER ON IN THE RELAY IT WAS THE TURN OF SOME NEXT GENERATION BAGGIES TO DO THE HONOURS A LITTLE CLOSER TO HOME.

Sam Wilding (pictured), who plays for the Academy's Under-12s, ran through Great Wyrley, while Dominic Macgowan, who plays for the Under-12s' Shadow Squad, was the country's youngest torchbearer when he ran through Birmingham aged only 12 years and 25 days.

"There was quite a lot of focus on me because of my age," said Dominic. "It's quite weird for me to get my head round, but I'm enjoying the fame at the moment – hopefully it will last a little longer.

"I got nominated by the PE department at school and I think they picked me because I'm quite sporty. I was excited and shocked when I found out

I would be carrying the Olympic torch".

Year seven pupil, Sam, was equally excited.

"My mum, dad and brothers came along to watch and I was excited. My Olympic kit was a bit big – but I don't mind. The PE department at my school nominated me to carry the torch and they said that I was committed to my school work and sport. They were asked to pick somebody from my year group and they picked me. I'll probably show my torch off when I can but my dad says I can't take it anywhere on my own. I'm not allowed to take it to the park or anything!"

YOUNG OLYMPIANS

Craig was part of Team GB as they fought their way to the quarter-finals, only to be beaten in a penalty shoot out by South Korea, and he says that it was an experience he will never forget.

"It was an amazing experience to be part of an Olympic Games, especially with it being in this country. We were mainly away from the Olympic Village – but we did spend three nights there and we met several athletes from other countries.

"I've enjoyed working with Giggs, Bellamy, all the experienced pros and Stuart Pearce again. I think I've learnt a lot from them. There was great support wherever we went and it was nice to get on the pitch and be a proper part of it.

"Hopefully I can take a lot from the experience and bring it to the Albion. It's been a good experience for me. It was a once-in-a-lifetime opportunity to play in the Olympics in Britain. It ranks up there with my best achievements and it was a great honour to be a part of it."

Dawson also revealed how he ended up taking a spot-kick in the shootout with South Korea, which he comfortably converted.

"It was a tough, tough game against South Korea, we created a few chances but just couldn't get the winner in the end and they were a good strong, organised team. On the night they played well against us – and when it goes to penalties it's a lottery that can go either way, and unfortunately for Daniel Sturridge he missed.

"The players selected to take the penalties goes from the records the staff have – and I was right up there on the list, so I was told I was taking one. We took them in training every day and they record the stats.

"I missed a couple but we did take quite a few. I just picked my spot and stayed with it. It was my first penalty and a big stage for it! It was nice to see it strike the back of the net – and then it was even harder work watching!"

THE OLYMPIC EXPERIENCE!

THE OLYMPICS MADE A BIG IMPACT ON EVERYONE THIS SUMMER, AND RIGHT IN THE MIDDLE OF IT WAS A THROSTLE – CRAIG DAWSON.

ASK ME ANOTHER:
CHRIS BRUNT

If you could buy a ticket to any event in the world, what would it be?

That's a really tricky question but I'd like to go to a World Cup final one day. That might sound cheesy but I'd like to go and wouldn't really be bothered who was playing.

What is your favourite colour?

Blue. I don't know why. What can I say? I'm a typical boy, I just like blue.

Who was your first-ever 11-a-side football match for and in what position?

I think it would've been for the boys club St. Andrews and I played on the left wing.

What is your favourite other sport?

Golf: to watch and to play. But I'm not very good at playing it despite the golf lessons I've had.

What was your best and worst subject at school?

Aside from PE, which we weren't allowed to do at GCSE level for some reason, I was good at French and got an A* in my GCSE. My worst subject was IT because everyone wanted to get on the internet. But we weren't allowed, so it was boring and the technician knew when you'd snuck online so there was no getting away with it!

Which team did you support as a boy?

Manchester United, I followed in the footsteps of my older cousin.

What is your favourite item of clothing?

I don't really have any one thing but I buy a lot of trainers so I wouldn't be able to do without those. My wife always tells me off for buying them.

WHEN IT WAS ANNOUNCED THAT SIMON COX HAD WON THE GOAL OF THE SEASON AWARD FOR HIS BELTER AGAINST TOTTENHAM IN THE 2010/11 CAMPAIGN, JAMES MORRISON COULD FEEL A BIT UPSET AT LOSING OUT WITH THE SCREAMER HE'D SCORED AGAINST MANCHESTER UNITED.

But Robert the Bruce's words of "If at first you don't succeed, try, try again" obviously struck a chord with the Scottish international, so this year, he just got on with the job of scoring an even better goal.

It came up at Blackburn, just before Christmas, a searing volley that flew through the penalty area and into the top corner.

So no arguments this time – James Morrison, this is your trophy!

WHAT A GOAL!

ON YOUR MARKS, GET SET...

PRE-SEASON IS SUPPOSED TO BE A TIME OF TORTURE, WHEN PLAYERS COME BACK FROM A FEW WEEKS OF REST, ONLY TO BE WHIPPED BACK INTO SHAPE BY LOTS OF LONG RUNS, HOURS OF STRETCHING AND TWISTING, AND GAME AFTER GAME OF FOOTBALL.

The Throstles spent a lot of this pre-season out in Sweden, getting themselves fit, ready and raring to go for the new challenges ahead under Steve Clarke. If you ask them, they'll tell you it was all hard work, non-stop.

Funny, they seem to be enjoying themselves in these pictures...

WEST BROMWICH ALBION

Swedbank Stadion

BAGGIES ON TOUR · SWEDEN 2012
MALMÖ 🤝 WEST BROM
STADION SWEDBANK · 19TH JULY

MALMÖ STADION

45

GOALKEEPER BEN FOSTER WAS A POPULAR MAN AT THE HAWTHORNS LAST SEASON – AND HE WASN'T EVEN OUR PLAYER THEN!

Big Ben won the Players' Player of the Season and Supporters' Player of the Season awards as well as the Disabled Supporters' Club's award to boot after an incredible season on loan with the Throstles.

Ben took 62% of the vote in the club's official Facebook poll and throughout the summer, Albion supporters were asking just when we were going to sign him up.

We did just that at the end of June just before the players returned for pre-season training, bringing him across Birmingham from St Andrew's and making him a full-time Baggie. Ben was thrilled to finally get the deal done.

"This is my club and hopefully I'm going to settle in and have the best years of my career here," said Foster.

"It's going to be strange to feel so settled. I've been on loan for many years of my career, so it's nice to know that this is my club now. This is a huge moment in my life, and in my career.

PLAYER OF THE SEASON! AND WE'RE KEEPING HIM!

"The decision to come here on loan last season was a chance to stay in the Midlands, but working with Roy Hodgson and Dean Kiely were other big factors.

"As it turned out it couldn't have really gone much better. I managed to play virtually every game, apart from missing that last game of the season, which was really frustrating as there was genuinely nothing I could do about it.

"I've got two young kids who are three and four and they're going to be going to school soon. I suppose fans don't always see that side of things, but that has a huge bearing on me because I'm a family-orientated person.

"My family is a massive part of my life, so it's very nice to be able to settle down and know that we're going to be here for a prolonged period of time."

If you could buy a ticket to any event in the world, what would it be?

The World Cup final. Any teams but I'd really like to see Brazil versus Spain.

What has been your most embarrassing moment?

There's quite a few to choose from and most of them you can't print but singing in front of the first team at Middlesbrough when I was younger because I hadn't cleaned the first team's boots, was really awful. A few of us did the 'Macarena'.

Tell us a joke...

Two goldfish in a tank, one says to the other 'do you know how to drive this thing?'

What is your favourite colour?

Red. Too much time at Boro probably!

What was your best and worst subject at school?

My best was PE and my worst was French. I didn't like the teacher and I didn't find it easy so I used to try everything I could to get out of it.

Would you like to be a manager one day?

I know I want to stay in football when I finish playing so it's definitely a possibility.

If you were cooking to impress, what dish would you select?

Steak and chips with some fresh vegetables. It's simple, tasty and easy to do.

ASK ME ANOTHER:
JAMES MORRISON

Jacob is no stranger to wearing blue and white stripes, even if Argentina's are a lighter shade of blue, and the arrival of the 25 year old gives new head coach plenty of welcome selection headaches in the middle of the pitch.

"He is an Argentina international with a real desire to prove himself in the Premier League and it's great to have him on board" said Steve Clarke.

"Claudio's got different qualities to the other midfielders we've got at the club and he should complement the squad very well.

"It will take him a little bit of time to adjust to the demands of the English game and he's also got to learn our language, but we hope to have him up and running for the start of the season."

As you can see from these pictures taken out in Sweden immediately after he arrived, we didn't waste any time in putting him through his paces!

MAN IN THE MIDDLE

ALBION INCREASED OUR MIDFIELD STRENGTH IN THE SUMMER BY SIGNING ARGENTINE INTERNATIONAL CLAUDIO YACOB FROM RACING CLUB DE AVELLANEDA AND IMMEDIATELY GRANTING HIM THE NUMBER FIVE SHIRT.

PLAYER PROFILES

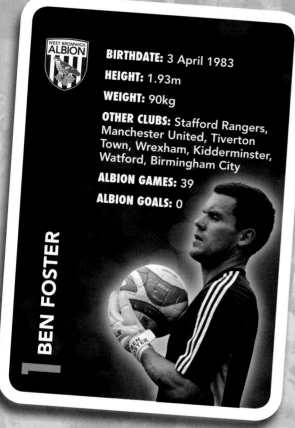

BIRTHDATE: 3 April 1983

HEIGHT: 1.93m

WEIGHT: 90kg

OTHER CLUBS: Stafford Rangers, Manchester United, Tiverton Town, Wrexham, Kidderminster, Watford, Birmingham City

ALBION GAMES: 39

ALBION GOALS: 0

1 BEN FOSTER

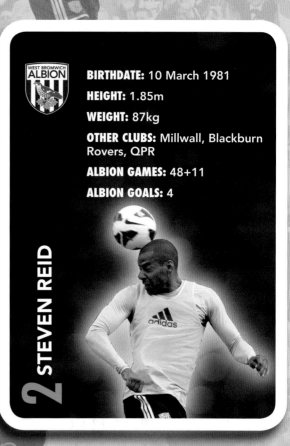

BIRTHDATE: 10 March 1981

HEIGHT: 1.85m

WEIGHT: 87kg

OTHER CLUBS: Millwall, Blackburn Rovers, QPR

ALBION GAMES: 48+11

ALBION GOALS: 4

2 STEVEN REID

BEN FOSTER WON ALBION'S "PLAYER OF THE SEASON" AWARD IN 2011/12 AFTER AN EPIC SEASON BETWEEN THE POSTS WHILE ON LOAN FROM BIRMINGHAM CITY.

The well-travelled former Manchester United goalkeeper made his switch from Birmingham a permanent one in June 2012 when he became Steve Clarke's first signing as Albion's new Head Coach. Foster missed only one game last season, the final one at The Hawthorns against Arsenal, and also played in Albion's two FA Cup ties.

STEVEN'S EXPERIENCE AT THE TOP LEVEL – FOR BOTH BLACKBURN AND IRELAND – HAS BEEN A CRUCIAL QUALITY FOR ALBION EVER SINCE HE FIRST CAME HERE ON LOAN DURING THE PROMOTION WINNING SEASON UNDER ROBERTO DI MATTEO.

Roy Hodgson made him a regular in his side as soon as he joined the club, Reid making the right-back position his own, although a couple of injuries restricted him to just over half a season's worth of games last term.

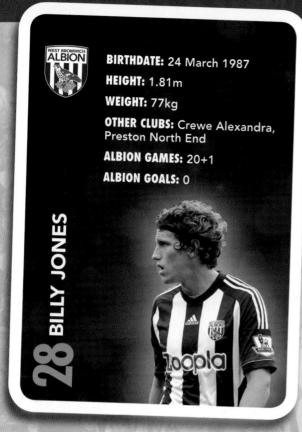

BIRTHDATE: 24 March 1987

HEIGHT: 1.81m

WEIGHT: 77kg

OTHER CLUBS: Crewe Alexandra, Preston North End

ALBION GAMES: 20+1

ALBION GOALS: 0

28 BILLY JONES

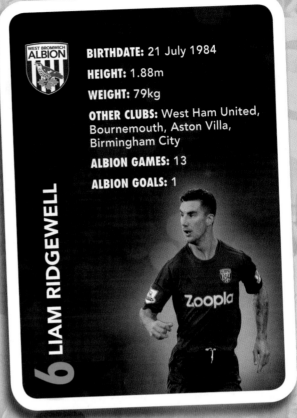

BIRTHDATE: 21 July 1984

HEIGHT: 1.88m

WEIGHT: 79kg

OTHER CLUBS: West Ham United, Bournemouth, Aston Villa, Birmingham City

ALBION GAMES: 13

ALBION GOALS: 1

6 LIAM RIDGEWELL

BILLY INITIALLY GOT HIS CHANCE IN THE SIDE WHEN HE REPLACED NICKY SHOREY AS LEFT-BACK AGAINST WOLVES AT THE HAWTHORNS LAST SEASON, SETTING UP CHRIS BRUNT'S GOAL EARLY IN THE GAME.

His longest run in the team came just after Christmas when he came on as a substitute in his more regular right-back place in the game up at Newcastle. He and Steven Reid have since enjoyed a close fight for that position in the Albion team.

LIAM RIDGWELL SIGNED FOR ALBION IN JANUARY 2012, GIVING US EXTRA STRENGTH IN DEFENCE WITH HIS ABILITY TO PLAY AT BOTH LEFT-BACK AND CENTRE-HALF IF REQUIRED, FILLING BOTH POSITIONS AT VARIOUS TIMES LAST SEASON.

Liam has also played for Aston Villa and Birmingham City and so is a something of a veteran of midlands football. His first goal for the club came in the 3-0 win over Blackburn Rovers at The Hawthorns.

PLAYER PROFILES

GARETH JOINED THE CLUB IN THE SUMMER OF 2011 AND HAD A WRETCHED START TO HIS TIME WITH THE CLUB AS HE SUFFERED FROM ILLNESS WHICH MADE A REAL MESS OF HIS PRE-SEASON PREPARATIONS.

It took him a while to get into the team after that, but once he gave a commanding display at Everton in the League Cup, there was no shifting him! He came third in Albion's Facebook "Player of the Season" poll and continued to win caps for Northern Ireland.

JONAS ENDED ANOTHER FINE SEASON AT THE HEART OF THE ALBION DEFENCE BY PLAYING IN THE EUROPEAN CHAMPIONSHIPS FOR SWEDEN, STARTING IN THEIR LAST TWO GROUP GAMES AGAINST ENGLAND AND FRANCE.

The giant centre-half has scored many important goals for Albion as well as being a tower of strength in defence, but none of his previous goals were more important than the ones he scored away from against Aston Villa and Wolves last season to help us earn two great wins.

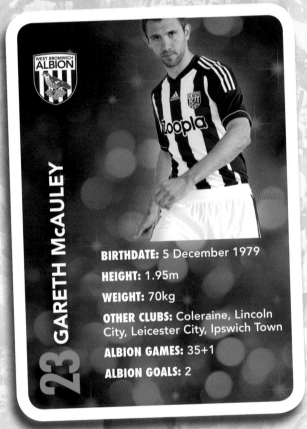

23 GARETH McAULEY

BIRTHDATE: 5 December 1979

HEIGHT: 1.95m

WEIGHT: 70kg

OTHER CLUBS: Coleraine, Lincoln City, Leicester City, Ipswich Town

ALBION GAMES: 35+1

ALBION GOALS: 2

3 JONAS OLSSON

BIRTHDATE: 10 March 1983

HEIGHT: 1.93m

WEIGHT: 84kg

OTHER CLUBS: Landskrona, NEC Nijmegen

ALBION GAMES: 135+1

ALBION GOALS: 11

BIRTHDATE: 6 May 1990

HEIGHT: 1.88m

WEIGHT: 83kg

OTHER CLUBS: Rochdale

ALBION GAMES: 9+3

ALBION GOALS: 0

25 CRAIG DAWSON

30 GABRIEL TAMAS

BIRTHDATE: 9 November 1983

HEIGHT: 1.88m

WEIGHT: 79kg

OTHER CLUBS: Dinamo Bucharest, Celta Vigo, Auxerre, Galatasaray

ALBION GAMES: 55+7

ALBION GOALS: 2

CRAIG ENJOYED HIS FIRST FULL SEASON AT THE HAWTHORNS AFTER HIS SWITCH FROM ROCHDALE, PLAYING A NUMBER OF GAMES AROUND THE CHRISTMAS AND NEW YEAR PERIOD AFTER JONAS OLSSON DROPPED OUT OF THE TEAM THROUGH INJURY.

The young centre-half has been a regular for England's Under 21s team and Stuart Pearce also selected him for the Team GB squad for the 2012 Olympics this summer.

ROMANIA'S GABRIEL TAMAS HAD A DIFFICULT SEASON LAST YEAR AFTER HE GOT A RED CARD AFTER THE GAME AWAY AT NORWICH CITY.

By the time he had served his suspension, Gareth McAuley had got into the team and he kept him out for much of the season, although Gabriel did come back and play an important part in the team at left-back on occasion, notably in our famous win away at Stoke City.

PLAYER PROFILES

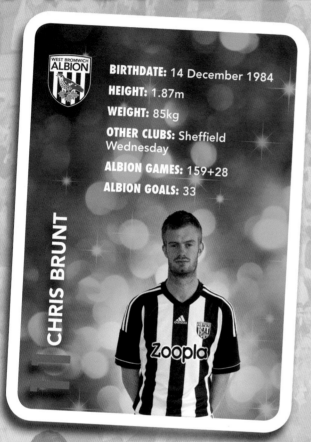

CHRIS BRUNT

BIRTHDATE: 14 December 1984

HEIGHT: 1.87m

WEIGHT: 85kg

OTHER CLUBS: Sheffield Wednesday

ALBION GAMES: 159+28

ALBION GOALS: 33

JEROME THOMAS

BIRTHDATE: 23 March 1983

HEIGHT: 1.77m

WEIGHT: 74kg

OTHER CLUBS: Arsenal, Charlton Athletic, QPR, Portsmouth

ALBION GAMES: 84+10

ALBION GOALS: 13

THE CLUB CAPTAIN SUFFERED A NASTY ANKLE INJURY ON NEW YEAR'S DAY 2012 IN THE GAME AGAINST EVERTON, BUT EVEN THOUGH HE MISSED A COUPLE OF MONTHS THROUGH INJURY, HE WAS AN INFLUENTIAL PLAYER FOR THE THROSTLES AGAIN LAST SEASON.

He has played more games and scored more goals for Albion than anybody else at the club since he joined us in the summer of 2007 to play his part in Tony Mowbray's promotion winning team.

JEROME IS CLOSING IN ON 100 GAMES IN HIS THREE SEASONS AT THE HAWTHORNS SINCE JOINING US FROM PORTSMOUTH.

After starting his career at Arsenal, Jerome really made his name at Charlton where his raw pace regularly troubled top defenders. A period of injury saw him suffer a couple of pretty mixed seasons, but since coming to The Hawthorns, his footballing health has been greatly improved and he has been back to his best form.

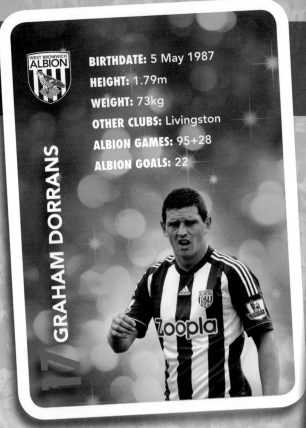

BIRTHDATE: 5 May 1987

HEIGHT: 1.79m

WEIGHT: 73kg

OTHER CLUBS: Livingston

ALBION GAMES: 95+28

ALBION GOALS: 22

17 GRAHAM DORRANS

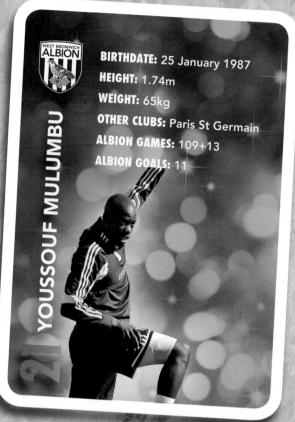

BIRTHDATE: 25 January 1987

HEIGHT: 1.74m

WEIGHT: 65kg

OTHER CLUBS: Paris St Germain

ALBION GAMES: 109+13

ALBION GOALS: 11

21 YOUSSOUF MULUMBU

AFTER SETTING THE CHAMPIONSHIP ON FIRE IN HIS FIRST FULL SEASON AT THE HAWTHORNS, HIS GOALS PROPELLING ALBION TOWARDS PROMOTION IN 2009/10, GRAHAM HAS HAD A COUPLE OF DIFFICULT SEASONS IN THE PREMIER LEAGUE AS A SERIES OF NIGGLING INJURIES HAVE STOPPED HIM GETTING A CONSISTENT RUN OF GAMES IN THE FIRST TEAM.

He finally managed to get a more regular place in the team in the second half of 2011/12 and goals against Stoke, QPR and Arsenal were reminders of the great ability he has.

FANS FAVOURITE YOUSSOUF MULUMBU WENT PAST THE 100 GAME MARK FOR ALBION DURING LAST SEASON, THOUGH HE DIDN'T QUITE LIVE UP TO THE GOALSCORING STANDARDS HE HAD SET IN THE PREVIOUS SEASON WHEN HE WON THE "PLAYER OF THE SEASON" AWARD.

The Congolese midfielder continued to be everywhere on the field at once, his energy and all action style making him one of the best defensive midfielders in the whole of the Premier League. Better than Kaka? Obviously!

PLAYER PROFILES

BIRTHDATE: 25 May 1986
HEIGHT: 1.78m
WEIGHT: 64kg
OTHER CLUBS: Middlesbrough
ALBION GAMES: 118+32
ALBION GOALS: 18

7 JAMES MORRISON

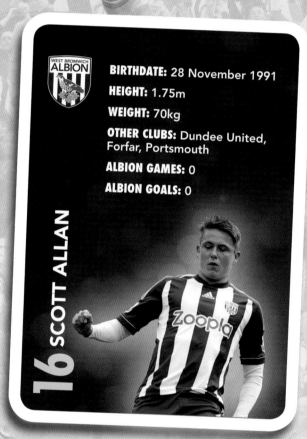

BIRTHDATE: 28 November 1991
HEIGHT: 1.75m
WEIGHT: 70kg
OTHER CLUBS: Dundee United, Forfar, Portsmouth
ALBION GAMES: 0
ALBION GOALS: 0

16 SCOTT ALLAN

DESPITE A COUPLE OF INJURIES, JAMES ENJOYED PROBABLY HIS BEST SEASON AT THE ALBION, TAKING HIS TOTAL OF APPEARANCES UP TO 150 BY SEASON'S END IN THE FIVE YEARS HE HAS BEEN HERE.

Such was James' form that had he not missed half a dozen games in the final few weeks of the campaign, he might have pushed Ben Foster much closer as "Player of the Season". He ended up runner-up in that race, but he did carry off the "Goal of the Season" trophy for his scorcher against Blackburn.

SCOTT ALLAN WAS A JANUARY 2012 SIGNING FROM DUNDEE UNITED, THE MIDFIELDER QUICKLY GOING OUT ON LOAN TO PORTSMOUTH AS THEY TRIED TO FIGHT OFF RELEGATION FROM THE CHAMPIONSHIP LAST TERM.

An under-21 international with Scotland, he has been a regular in the SPL for Dundee United before Albion moved in to bring him south. He will be hoping this is going to be his breakthrough season at The Hawthorns.

24 PETER ODEMWINGIE

BIRTHDATE: 15 July 1981

HEIGHT: 1.81m

WEIGHT: 75kg

OTHER CLUBS: Bendel Insurance, La Louviere, Lille, Lokomotiv Moscow

ALBION GAMES: 56+8

ALBION GOALS: 26

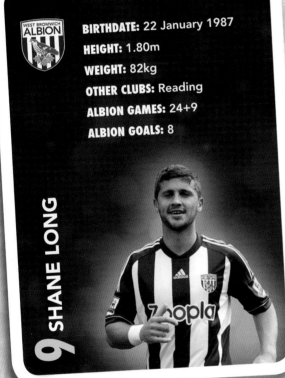

9 SHANE LONG

BIRTHDATE: 22 January 1987

HEIGHT: 1.80m

WEIGHT: 82kg

OTHER CLUBS: Reading

ALBION GAMES: 24+9

ALBION GOALS: 8

THE NIGERIAN INTERNATIONAL HAD ANOTHER GREAT SEASON FOR THE BAGGIES, FINISHING AS OUR TOP SCORER FOR THE SECOND SEASON IN A ROW, BRINGING HIS GOALS TALLY TO 26 FOR THE CLUB.

He scored only our third hat-trick in the Premier League when he destroyed the Wolves at Molineux in our 5-1 win and became the first man to score double figures for us in two separate Premiership seasons, and let's see if he can make it three in a row this year!

SHANE HAD A FABULOUS START TO HIS ALBION CAREER, SCORING IN EACH OF HIS FIRST TWO GAMES, AND AGAINST PRETTY DECENT OPPOSITION TOO – MANCHESTER UNITED AND CHELSEA!

Illness and injury around Christmas and the New Year knocked him off his stride a little bit but he ended the season in great form, scoring against Arsenal, before heading to the European Championships where he enjoyed two substitute appearances for the Irish.

PLAYER PROFILES

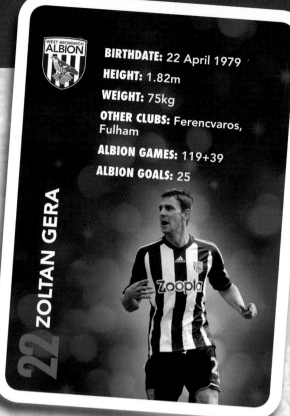

ZOLTAN GERA
22

BIRTHDATE: 22 April 1979
HEIGHT: 1.82m
WEIGHT: 75kg
OTHER CLUBS: Ferencvaros, Fulham
ALBION GAMES: 119+39
ALBION GOALS: 25

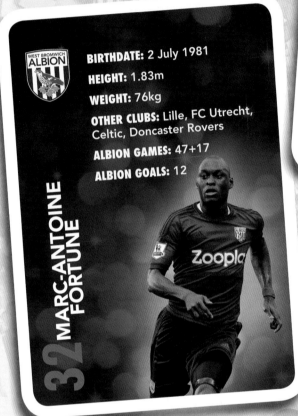

MARC-ANTOINE FORTUNE
32

BIRTHDATE: 2 July 1981
HEIGHT: 1.83m
WEIGHT: 76kg
OTHER CLUBS: Lille, FC Utrecht, Celtic, Doncaster Rovers
ALBION GAMES: 47+17
ALBION GOALS: 12

ZOLTAN GERA'S ALBION RETURN WAS CUT VERY SHORT LAST SEASON WHEN HE SUFFERED A KNEE INJURY IN ONLY HIS THIRD GAME BACK IN THE STRIPES.

After working very hard to get fit again since then, Zoltan will be looking forward to getting back into Steve Clarke's team and making up for lost time from last season. Zoltan was part of the "Great Escape" team of 2005 and the promotion winners of 2008, so he'll be looking forward to another epic season to add to his Albion collection!

MARC-ANTOINE FORTUNE SPENT THE EARLY PART OF LAST SEASON OUT ON LOAN AT DONCASTER ROVERS AND IT SEEMED AS IF HIS ALBION CAREER MIGHT BE OVER.

But after Christmas, he became a central part of the team with a string of excellent performances at centre-forward, starting with his display in the win at Stoke. Holding the ball well up front to help his colleagues get forward, he also helped himself to a few goals too.

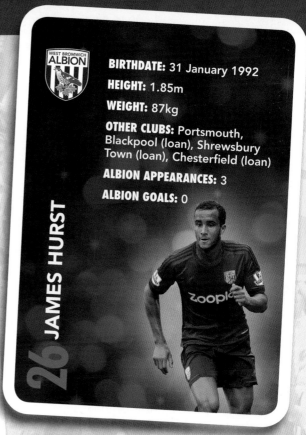

BIRTHDATE: 31 January 1992

HEIGHT: 1.85m

WEIGHT: 87kg

OTHER CLUBS: Portsmouth, Blackpool (loan), Shrewsbury Town (loan), Chesterfield (loan)

ALBION APPEARANCES: 3

ALBION GOALS: 0

26 JAMES HURST

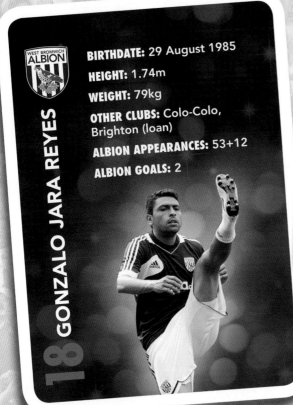

BIRTHDATE: 29 August 1985

HEIGHT: 1.74m

WEIGHT: 79kg

OTHER CLUBS: Colo-Colo, Brighton (loan)

ALBION APPEARANCES: 53+12

ALBION GOALS: 2

18 GONZALO JARA REYES

JAMES WON ALBION'S YOUNG PLAYER OF THE SEASON AWARD IN 2010/11.

He spent most of last season out on loan at various clubs including Blackpool, Shrewsbury Town and Chesterfield, with whom he won the Football League Trophy at Wembley in March 2012 when they beat Swindon 2-0. James is a very talented right-back who always seems to have plenty of time on the ball, and he's pretty quick when he joins up with the attack too!

GONZO SPENT A PART OF LAST SEASON OUT ON LOAN AT THE OTHER ALBION – BRIGHTON & HOVE ALBION – AS STEVEN REID AND BILLY JONES MANAGED TO DOMINATE THE RIGHT-BACK POSITION.

This season, he is back and trying to get into Steve Clarke's first team plans. The fact that he can play in either full-back position, at centre-half or even in midfield will surely give the Chilean an opportunity to impress he head coach somewhere along the line!

El Ghanassy, who can play on either wing and also as a striker, made his name in Belgium with his pace and trickery on the ball and won the first of his two full international caps against Finland in February 2011.

Head coach Steve Clarke said, "He is an exciting, young prospect who will hopefully add something different to our squad. This is a big move for Yassine and we'll have to be patient with him as he settles into a new country and gets to grips with the demands of the Barclays Premier League. But we believe he has got the raw talent to make an impact here."

Yassine sees himself as a player who can excite the supporters and said, "I like to run with the ball, and I promise the team some skills. I expect that if I play some games, a lot of people will come and love my skills, and I hope that some people in West Brom will come and watch.

"The Premier League is the best league in the world and I am very, very happy to be playing in this league. I'm going to be playing against the top teams in the world and I'm very, very happy and I'm very, very hungry. Albion have a very strong history and I'm very happy that I will be playing for this club."

A VERY NICE MAN FROM AA GENT!

BELGIAN INTERNATIONAL YASSINE EL GHANASSY WAS ONE OF ALBION'S SUMMER SIGNINGS, JOINING FROM AA GENT ON A SEASON LONG LOAN.

CROSSWORD

```
              Z O O P L A
      R     M         O
  T H E H A W T H O R N S
  O   I     R         G
  N   D     C   B           B
  Y       O D E M W I N G I E
  B         B             L
  R         E             L
G O A L S   M O O R E     Y
  O         F
  W         Z O L T A N
  N         S
            T
            E
        G A R E T H
```

WORDSEARCH

C	L	A	R	K	E	N	S	B	C	S
F	W	L	G	A	T	B	M	N	Y	H
K	T	B	I	J	O	N	E	S	U	A
G	G	I	S	A	K	F	T	E	X	N
R	L	O	Y	M	O	D	H	V	G	E
A	X	N	K	E	D	M	W	Q	K	Y
H	A	U	R	S	B	Y	I	K	D	C
A	M	N	E	L	R	L	C	Y	E	M
M	C	F	W	R	U	S	K	C	Q	U
E	U	A	B	W	N	T	H	B	O	H
L	F	H	A	W	T	H	O	R	N	S

QUIZ ANSWERS

P38 **BIG QUIZ**

1. John Osborne
2. 1930/31 – won the FA Cup & promotion to the top flight, a unique achievement
3. NEC Nijmegen
4. 279
5. Peter Odemwingie
6. Aston Villa & Birmingham City
7. Lee Marshall
8. True – we won eight in 2010/11
9. Five
10. Five
11. Real Madrid
12. Dennis Clarke
13. Marton Fulop
14. Arsenal
15. True – Peter Odemwingie in 2010/11
16. Portsmouth
17. Four
18. 1878
19. Three - Manchester United, Reading, Swansea City
20. Jesse Pennington

P28 **SPOT THE BALL**

CRABBIE'S ALCOH